The Book of
FEELS
&
WONDERS

BROOKS IMEL

LUMINARE PRESS
WWW.LUMINAREPRESS.COM

Luminare Press
442 Charnelton St.
Eugene, OR 97401
www.luminarepress.com

LCCN: 2020912805
ISBN: 978-1-64388-421-9

For Gwen

I see a foggy morning.

What do you see?

I see bright red flowers.
I feel inspired.

What do you feel?

I see a house, floating on the water.
I feel confused.
I wonder if it will sink.

What do you wonder?

I see a man in a blue shirt.

What do you see?

Claude Monet

I see two ships on the blue river.
I feel adventurous.

What do you feel?

I see a sunny day.
I feel happy.
I wonder if the sunflowers do too.

What do you wonder?

I see people watching
a horse race.

What do you see?

I see a fence.
I feel like jumping over it.

What do you feel?

I see a lily pond.
I feel curious.
I wonder if mermaids live in there.

What do you wonder?

I see a boy standing in the tall grass.

What do you see?

I see green trees.
I feel like climbing them.

What do you feel?

I see a boy playing with toys.
I feel like playing with him.
I wonder if he'd be my friend.

What do you wonder?

I see a horse-drawn carriage.

What do you see?

26

I see a fancy party.
I feel like dancing.

What do you feel?

I see a rowboat.
I feel like going out on the water.
I wonder how boats float.

What do you wonder?

I see lots of big, tall buildings.

What do you see?

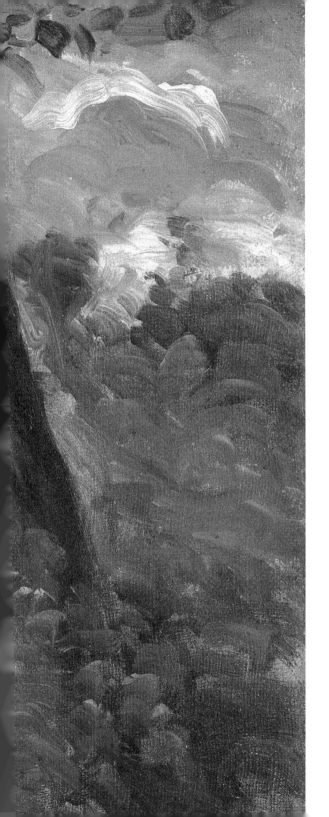

I see a windy day.
I feel like it's about to thunder.

What do you feel?

I see a man in a boat,
drifting across the water.
I feel sleepy.
I wonder if this is someone's dream.

What do you wonder?

The End

About the Impressionists

The paintings in this book are by artists who were part of a group called the Impressionists. The Impressionists painted in the 1800s, and many of them lived in Paris, France. In fact, some of them were friends, and they liked to paint the same kinds of subjects—mainly landscapes and scenes of everyday life. They were fascinated by light, and they liked to paint the same scenes at different times of day. They also loved to paint water, which often reflects light in interesting and beautiful ways.

What do you think is interesting and beautiful? If you could paint anything, what would it be?

Index of Paintings

Claude Monet, *Morning Haze,* 1888 1-2

Claude Monet, *The Artist's Garden in Argenteuil*
(A Corner of the Garden with Dahlias), 1873 3-4

Claude Monet, *Bridge at Argenteuil on a Gray Day,* c. 1876 5-6

Claude Monet, *Sainte-Adresse,* 1867 7-8

Claude Monet, *Ships Riding on the Seine at Rouen,* 1872/1873 9-10

Claude Monet, *The Artist's Garden at Vétheuil,* 1881 11-12

Edouard Manet, *At the Races,* c. 1875 13-14

Camille Pissarro, *The Fence,*1872 15-16

Claude Monet, *The Japanese Footbridge,* 1899 17-18

Claude Monet, *Woman with a Parasol - Madame Monet and Her Son,* 1875 19-20

Auguste Renoir, *View of Monte Carlo from Cap Martin,* c. 1884 21-22

Auguste Renoir, *Child with Toys - Gabrielle and the Artist's Son, Jean,* 1895-1896 23-24

Camille Pissarro, *Boulevard des Italiens, Morning, Sunlight,* 1897 25-26

Edouard Manet, *Masked Ball at the Opera,* 1873 27-28

Auguste Renoir, *Oarsmen at Chatou,* 1879 29-30

Auguste Renoir, *Pont Neuf, Paris,* 1872 31-32

Auguste Renoir, *Landscape between Storms,* 1874/1875 33-34

Claude Monet, *The Houses of Parliament, Sunset,* 1902 35-36

CPSIA information can be obtained
at www.ICGtesting.com
Printed in the USA
BVHW051320270820
587434BV00040BA/1839

Wild
WEATHER
Tales

3 STORIES IN 1!

Based on the television series
created by Craig Bartlett

Grosset & Dunlap
An Imprint of Penguin Group (USA) Inc.

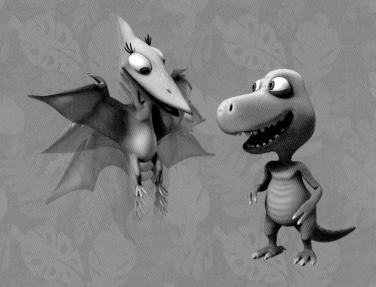

GROSSET & DUNLAP
Published by the Penguin Group
Penguin Group (USA) Inc., 375 Hudson Street, New York, New York 10014, USA
Penguin Group (Canada), 90 Eglinton Avenue East, Suite 700, Toronto, Ontario M4P 2Y3, Canada
(a division of Pearson Penguin Canada Inc.)
Penguin Books Ltd., 80 Strand, London WC2R 0RL, England
Penguin Group Ireland, 25 St. Stephen's Green, Dublin 2, Ireland
(a division of Penguin Books Ltd.)
Penguin Group (Australia), 707 Collins Street, Melbourne, Victoria 3008, Australia
(a division of Pearson Australia Group Pty. Ltd.)
Penguin Books India Pvt. Ltd., 11 Community Centre, Panchsheel Park, New Delhi—110 017, India
Penguin Group (NZ), 67 Apollo Drive, Rosedale, Auckland 0632, New Zealand
(a division of Pearson New Zealand Ltd.)
Penguin Books, Rosebank Office Park, 181 Jan Smuts Avenue, Parktown North 2193, South Africa
Penguin China, B7 Jaiming Center, 27 East Third Ring Road North, Chaoyang District, Beijing 100020, China

Penguin Books Ltd., Registered Offices: 80 Strand, London WC2R 0RL, England

™ & © 2013 The Jim Henson Company. JIM HENSON'S mark & logo, DINOSAUR TRAIN mark & logo,
characters and elements are trademarks of The Jim Henson Company. All Rights Reserved.
Published by Grosset & Dunlap, a division of Penguin Young Readers Group, 345 Hudson Street, New York, New York 10014.
GROSSET & DUNLAP is a trademark of Penguin Group (USA) Inc. Manufactured in China.

The PBS KIDS logo is a registered mark of the Public Broadcasting Service and is used with permission.

http://pbskids.org/dinosaurtrain

The publisher does not have any control over and does not assume any
responsibility for author or third-party websites or their content.

ISBN 978-0-448-46468-8   10 9 8 7 6 5 4 3 2 1

ALWAYS LEARNING

PEARSON

Dry Times at Pteranodon Terrace

It was a hot day at Pteranodon Terrace. Buddy and Don thought it would be fun to play in the water.

"Hey, Buddy!" Don said. "Watch me jump into that water hole over there!"

Don took a running start and headed
straight toward the water hole. He jumped
up and was ready to make a big splash.

"Diiiiinoballl!" he shouted as he landed
with a thud in a dry, empty hole.

Buddy ran over to Don, who looked a little bit confused.

"What happened to the water?" Buddy asked.

"It's gone!" Don replied. "This was a water hole. But now there's no water, so it's just a hole."

Buddy and Don ran back to the nest to
tell everyone what had happened.

"Mom! Dad! Shiny! Tiny! Don tried to
splash into that water hole over there . . .
but all the water's gone! It's just a dry hole!"
Buddy said.

"That's what happens when it doesn't rain for several weeks," Mr. Pteranodon said. "Sometimes a long dry spell happens. It's called a drought."

"How about we turn this drought into a family adventure?" Mrs. Pteranodon asked. "We could go camping. There's plenty of water at the Big Pond."

The family headed to the Dinosaur Train.
It would take them to the Big Pond.

Mr. Conductor explained droughts to the kids.

"It's a problem with the water cycle. Normally, rain falls to the earth. Over time, heat sends water back up into the sky. That water turns into clouds," he said.

"But sometimes the water in the clouds
doesn't come back down as rain right
away," he continued.

Buddy knew that was a problem because
living things need water to survive.

"I know what'll bring a big rain— a rain dance!" Don said.

The family watched as Don danced around the train. When he finished, he looked out the window of the train. But it was still a bright sunny day outside.

Once they arrived at the Big Pond, Mr. and Mrs. Pteranodon began setting up camp. Don practiced his moves for the rain dance as the other kids played in the sand.

Buddy looked up at the sky. He was worried that the drought would hit the Big Pond soon. Then he had an idea.

"What if we all do the rain dance?" he asked.

"That's a great idea, Buddy!"
Mr. Pteranodon said.
Everyone got up and danced with Don.
Then Tiny looked up at the sky and noticed
clouds coming in.

After a few minutes of dancing, the sky
filled with dark clouds. Don put out his
hand.

"Hmm, it feels like rain," he said.

Suddenly, a few drops of rain started to
fall on them!

"It's raining! It's raining!" Don yelled.
"We did it!"

His brother and sisters cheered and danced with him in the rain. Mr. and Mrs. Pteranodon smiled and watched their happy children.

BIG
Storm at Pteranodon Terrace

The wind was blowing hard outside the family's nest.

"Can we go out and play?" Tiny asked.

Mrs. Pteranodon said okay, but warned them not to go flying.

Buddy and Don ran back to the nest.

They watched as Mr. Pteranodon made a crash landing. He was having trouble flying in the wind.

"Whoa! That is some crazy wind!" he said.

"Well, when's all this wind and rain going to end?" Buddy and Don asked their father.

"The rain is important for the plants! You should enjoy a little rain now that it's finally here," he said.

"With this wind picking up, it's turning into quite a storm!" Mr. Pteranodon continued.
Buddy peeked his head out from under the leaves. "How strong is the wind?" he asked.

"Strong enough to blow away the nest!"
Mr. Pteranodon replied.
The kids couldn't believe it. "Blow away
the nest?" they all said at the same time.

"Don't worry," Mrs. Pteranodon said, trying to comfort them. "Storms are part of nature."

"Just like rain!" Shiny added.

"That's right," Mrs. Pteranodon said. "The storm will pass, and then things will return to normal."

"But we need to keep ourselves safe during a storm this big," Mr. Pteranodon said. "Okay, team! Everybody take your favorite thing to play with—we'll stick together and move toward those trees."

Buddy and Don went exploring and found a big cave after falling into one of Don's holes. Don was worried he would get in trouble because his parents had warned him not to play in the holes during the storm.

But they weren't mad at him at all. Mr. Pteranodon grinned as he looked around at the cave.

"I think you have discovered the perfect place for us to ride out this storm!" he said to Don.

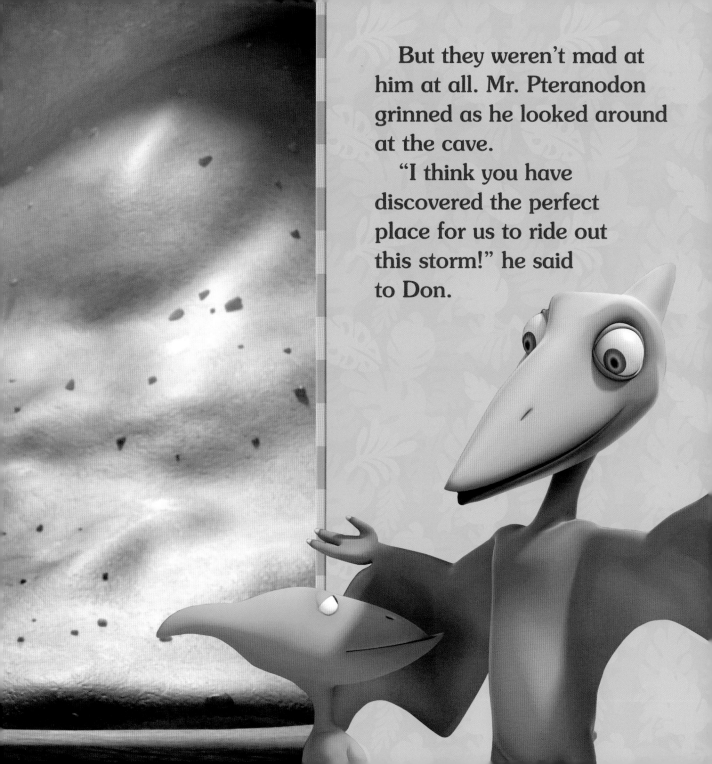

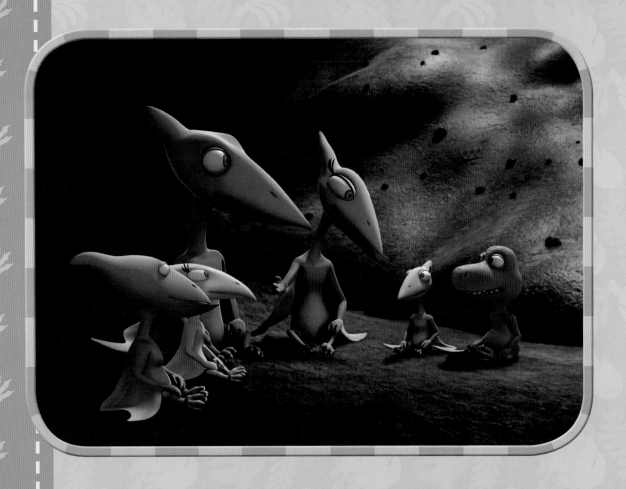

They could hear the wind blowing outside.
"Thank goodness Buddy and Don
discovered this cave!" Mrs. Pteranodon said.
"I feel so much better with you kids down
here rather than just being under
the trees."

Once the storm ended, they headed home. But when they reached the top of the cliff, they saw that there were only a few sticks where the nest used to be!

Buddy and the others were upset, but Mr. Pteranodon just smiled and said, "All right, Team Pteranodon! You know what it's time for?"

The kids jumped up and down. "Time to build a new nest!" they cheered.

Rafting across the Sea

Mr. and Mrs. Pteranodon cleared away
the branches that had been knocked down
in the storm. Buddy and Tiny wanted to
help, too. They found some big leaves and
started to sweep up the mess.

Shiny looked out at the ocean. She could see something floating in the water. It was on a giant wave and was headed right for the shore.

The kids were excited to see a large turtle slowly climb off a raft. "Hi, my name is Aidan Adocus," he said.

A small furry animal was sitting on his shell.

"Hi, I'm Tommy Ptilodus," he said.

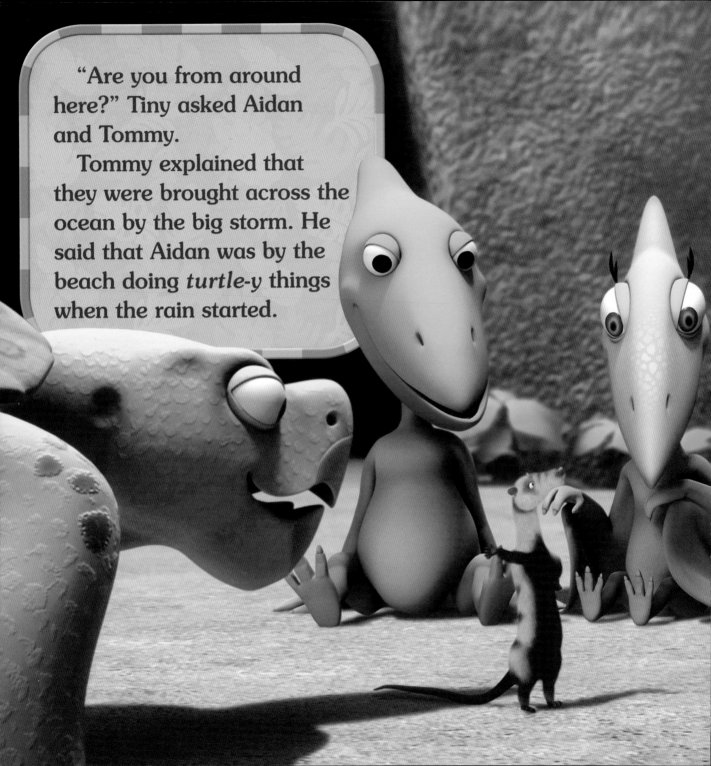

"Are you from around here?" Tiny asked Aidan and Tommy.

Tommy explained that they were brought across the ocean by the big storm. He said that Aidan was by the beach doing *turtle-y* things when the rain started.

Before Aidan knew it, the storm had washed him out to sea. Luckily, he saw a raft made of branches that had tangled together floating in the water. He climbed on and waited for the storm to end.

Tommy hopped onto the raft. "I'd been blown out to sea by the storm, too," he said, "and didn't know what I'd do."

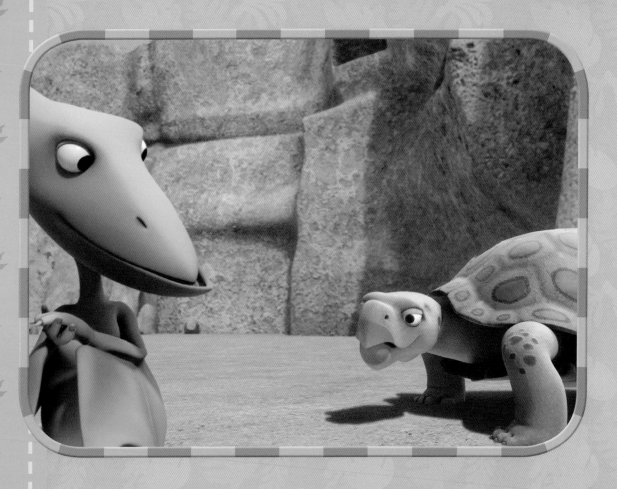

"Yep, here we are . . . far away from home . . . with no way to get back," Aidan said. He was afraid that he would never see his own beach again.

Buddy had a great idea. "I know exactly
how you can get back home!" he said.
He and Tiny exchanged a look and then
both yelled, "The Dinosaur Train!"

Aidan was really excited. "I've never been on the Dinosaur Train before," he said. "I prefer to stay on my beach."

Buddy was surprised. "We ride the Dinosaur Train all the time."

"I was thinking . . . ," Shiny said.
"We've never been to where you're from.
We never even knew there were beaches
anywhere else!"

Aidan and Tommy invited them all to come for a visit. The kids really wanted to see where their new friends lived. But they had to ask their parents first.

"Can we go, Mom and Dad?" they asked.

Mr. and Mrs. Pteranodon were happy
to take the kids to see where Aidan and
Tommy lived. Once they got there, Aidan
took them right to his beach.

They spent the whole day laughing and playing on the beach. It was the most fun they'd had in a while. The big storm started out scary but brought them the greatest gift of all—wonderful new friends.